Mattie

MARSHA WILSON CHALL

Illustrated by Barbara Lehman

AN AVON CAMELOT BOOK

If you purchased this book without a cover, you should be aware that this book is stolen property. It was reported as "unsold and destroyed" to the publisher, and neither the author nor the publisher has received any payment for this "stripped book."

To my two kids,
Lindsay and Robbie,
and to brothers and sisters
everywhere

AVON BOOKS
A division of
The Hearst Corporation
1350 Avenue of the Americas
New York, New York 10019

Text copyright © 1992 by Marsha Wilson Chall
Illustrations copyright © 1992 by Barbara Lehman
Published by arrangement with William Morrow and Company, Inc.
Library of Congress Catalog Card Number: 91-30425
ISBN: 0-380-72116-3
RL: 2.3

All rights reserved, which includes the right to reproduce this book or portions thereof in any form whatsoever except as provided by the U.S. Copyright Law. For information address Lothrop, Lee & Shepard Books, a division of William Morrow and Company, Inc., 1350 Avenue of the Americas, New York, New York 10019.

First Avon Camelot Printing: January 1994

CAMELOT TRADEMARK REG. U.S. PAT. OFF. AND IN OTHER COUNTRIES, MARCA REGISTRADA, HECHO EN U.S.A.

Printed in the U.S.A.

OPM 10 9 8 7 6 5 4 3 2 1

Avon Books are available at special quantity discounts for bulk purchases for sales promotions, premiums, fund raising or educational use. Special books, or book excerpts, can also be created to fit specific needs.

For details write or telephone the office of the Director of Special Markets, Avon Books, Dept. FP, 1350 Avenue of the Americas, New York, NY 10019, 1-800-238-0658.

Contents

1. The Chocolate-Ant Valentine
5

2. Kid for Sale — Any Amount
19

3. The Haircut
35

1. The Chocolate-Ant Valentine

Mattie couldn't wait to get back to school after winter vacation. She loved the second grade. It was a lot more grown-up than first grade. For one thing, the bathroom wasn't *in* the classroom. Second graders used the lavatory down the hall. Mattie liked that word, *lavatory.* Sometimes she said it four or five times a day. "May I please go to the lavatory, Mrs. Pritchard?" It was the longest word she knew. No wonder the lavatory door just said GIRLS.

Second-grade writing paper was more grown-up, too. It didn't look like a highway with dotted lines to print over and under. Second graders had that figured out. And it had a lot more lines to fill. Second graders could write a lot.

Second graders had their grown-up

teeth, too. Mattie's tongue stopped where it was supposed to, and straws stayed between her teeth instead of jabbing the top of her mouth. She could eat corn-on-the-cob again. By next year, she might even need braces!

Second-grade friends were friendlier. Mattie had memorized Darcy's and Felicia's phone numbers before Halloween, and they had memorized hers.

There was only one thing wrong with second grade: J. E. B. That stood for Jethro Ely Bonomo—Jeb, for short.

One morning Jeb put milk in Mattie's glue bottle. When she squeezed it, milk splashed all over her Four Food Groups collage. The chicken dripped milk onto the grapes. The grapes dripped milk onto the potatoes.

Jeb handed her a towel. "You forgot the Dairy Group," he said.

Another day Jeb put eggs in Mattie's boots. At recess she jumped into her snow pants, pulled her jacket and hat on, then slammed into her boots. SPLAT! Eggshells cracked beneath her feet. Egg yolks oozed between her toes. Mattie spent recess indoors, cleaning her socks and her boots.

Once, Jeb taped a long piece of toilet paper to the back of Mattie's jeans. She walked all the way through the lunch line with a white tail streaming behind her before she found out why everyone was laughing.

"Jeb teases you because he likes you," Mattie's mother said when Mattie complained after school that day.

Mattie almost shook her pigtails off. "No way!" she yelled. She wished she could teach Jeb a lesson.

One Friday afternoon, Mrs. Pritchard made an announcement. "Valentine's Day is just one week from today," she said. "This year we're going to do something special to celebrate." On her desk was a large box.

The entire second grade froze in their seats. Except for Jethro Ely Bonomo—he was picking his nose.

"Today each of you will draw from this box the name of a boy or girl in our class to be your Valentine's Secret Pal," Mrs. Pritchard went on. "Every day next week, you will secretly place a small treat or homemade gift on your Pal's desk. Then on Valentine's Day, you'll meet your Secret Pal, and you'll find out who's been giving *you* gifts."

Mattie tingled all over as she imagined the grand gifts she would get: cookies with red sugar sprinkles, homemade fudge, a heart-shaped chocolate cake with her name in white icing.

Mattie crossed her fingers over her heart for good luck, then reached into the box. She picked the third paper heart she touched. Closing her eyes tight, she slowly opened the heart. Then she took a deep breath and opened her eyes.

She almost choked! Her cheeks burned. Her stomach churned. Written on the paper heart was:

JETHRO ELY BONOMO

She ripped up the paper and stuffed the pieces between the pages of *Samantha Gets a New Friend.*

"Did you get someone you really like?" Felicia asked.

"Yeah," Mattie whispered. "Someone I'd really like to clobber."

On Monday morning, Mattie shook the tiny heart-shaped box on her desk. Something rattled inside. All day long she wondered what it could be. A necklace? Or candy? Maybe it was a pretty barrette.

Finally Mrs. Pritchard announced that it was time to open Valentine's gifts. Mattie crossed her fingers over her heart and opened the box.

"Oooh," she sighed. "It's beautiful!" She slipped the diamond ring over her finger.

"Someone must love you!" Darcy said.

"Do you really think so?" said Mattie.

Suddenly Lenny Preston hollered, "Look at Jeb's mouth! It's green!"

Mattie looked innocent. "What's wrong?" she said. "Oh, gross."

Green saliva oozed down Jeb's chin. He raced for the sink with his hand over his mouth. Mattie tried hard not to laugh.

Jeb reached for a paper towel. Then, suddenly, he stopped and turned. He straightened his back. He shot his arms out like a sleepwalker. He curled his hands into claws. He rolled his eyes. Then he charged at Darcy and Felicia. "Grrrr!" he growled.

Felicia crossed her arms over her head. Darcy jumped up and almost tripped over her desk.

"Where did you get that great trick gum, Jeb?" asked Lenny.

"From my Secret Pal. Pretty lucky, huh?" Jeb grinned a green grin.

"Rats!" Mattie whispered.

That night Mattie stayed at the dinner table after she'd finished eating.

"Lose your best friend?" asked her big sister, Abby.

Mattie balanced a spoon on the end of her nose. "No, I got a Secret Pal for Valentine's Day."

"Who'd you get?"

"It's a secret," Mattie said.

"I'm giving Tommy Berg cologne for Valentine's Day," said Abby.

"You're giving him cologne?" Mattie repeated. "Hmmmm. . . ."

Even my little brother could have taken that ribbon off, Mattie thought as Mrs. Pritchard finally cut it for Jeb. She popped a chocolate drop into her mouth. Too bad Jeb wouldn't get candy like she had today.

She watched closely as Jeb flipped the box open. "Wow!" he whispered. So far, so good.

The label said NATURAL MAN, in gold letters. Jeb unscrewed the top and inhaled. "Ugh!"

"What did ya get today, Jeb?" asked Lenny.

Jeb splashed Mattie's stinky concoction behind his ears. He rubbed it over his neck. He patted it on his hair. He spread it along his arms. "I got this special cologne. Don't you like it?"

Lenny held his nose.

"Peee-yoo!" Andy shouted. "You stink!"

"You've sure got a great Secret Pal!" said Stuart.

Mrs. Pritchard tapped her desk. "Jeb, your new cologne is very . . . distinctive, but I'm afraid I'll have to excuse you to go to the lavatory."

"Thank you, Mrs. Pritchard," said Jeb. At the door, he grinned and waved to the class.

Mattie watched the clock. Twenty-one minutes later, Jeb returned. He smelled okay *and* he'd missed the spelling test. Mattie kicked her desk.

Early Wednesday morning, Mattie darted between the empty desks in her classroom. She pulled a red foil cube from her pocket and quickly dropped it into Jeb's pencil tray. This will fix him, she thought as she wriggled into her seat.

At two o'clock Felicia and Darcy leaned over Mattie's shoulders.

"Oh, hurry, Mattie. Open your present," they squealed.

"In a minute," Mattie told them. "Jeb's opening his. Let's see what he has today."

Mattie smiled as Jeb bit into the chocolate candy. He swallowed. Good—he liked it. Now for the second bite—the surprise bite!

"Mmmmm," said Jeb. "This is the best chocolate-covered ant I've eaten all week!" The class was silent as Jeb chewed. *Crunch . . . Crunch . . . Crunch . . . Gulp!*

Lenny Preston cheered. "That was really cool, Jeb!"

The boys gathered around to admire the other half of the ant. Jeb smacked his lips all the way to the bus.

Mattie shrugged. Tomorrow was another day, and she was no quitter.

"You still haven't opened your present, Mattie," Felicia shouted over the grumbling of the bus's motor. Mattie quickly unwrapped the box. She felt her cheeks get warm.

"Oooh!" Darcy gushed. "Pink is my favorite color."

"I love the lace," said Felicia.

Darcy fastened the elegant bow in Mattie's hair. "Someone thinks you're beautiful, Mattie."

The next afternoon, after music, Mattie's desk bloomed with a dozen daffodils. Even Mrs. Pritchard was amazed.

"I bet you can hardly wait to meet your Secret Pal tomorrow," she said.

Mattie's heart raced. Tomorrow Jeb would meet his Secret Pal, too. She almost wished she could take back the present he was opening right now.

"Fangs! They're Dracula's fangs!" Lenny screamed.

Oh, no they're not, Mattie thought. They were her sister Abby's molars. The points were really long roots. Abby had eaten only ice cream for two days after Dr. Rathbone pulled them out to make room for her braces. Mattie had used tweezers to pick them up.

"Hey, Jeb," said Lenny. "I'll trade you this baseball card for those teeth."

"No, thanks," Jeb answered. "These are the greatest!"

Mattie scooped up her daffodils. That dope! How could he like all the stupid things she had given him? Worse yet, *all* the boys thought Jeb's presents were terrific! Everyone would think she liked him!

How could she face them all tomorrow? Maybe she could just skip school . . . but then she wouldn't meet *her* Secret Pal.

She crossed her fingers over her heart and trudged out to the bus.

Mattie wore the pink bow to school and studied especially hard on Valentine's Day. She wished it were a regular Friday— or that Jeb were out with the chicken pox.

"Hey, Mattie, aren't you going to deliver your Valentine's cards?" Darcy asked. "Everyone else is almost finished."

"In a minute," Mattie answered. "When I'm done with this worksheet."

"Weird," Darcy muttered.

After cleanup, Mrs. Pritchard clapped her hands. "It's time now to meet your Secret Pals!" she said.

Mattie's feet felt like they were stuck in cement. She couldn't get up from her desk.

"Are you okay?" Jeb asked.

"Not exactly," Mattie started. "Jeb, about those presents I gave you—"

"It was *you*?" Jeb interrupted. "They were great! My favorite was the chocolate-covered ant!"

"I was afraid of that." Mattie sighed as she searched the room for *her* Secret Pal, but everyone was matched up.

"You look real pretty in that pink bow, Mattie," Jeb whispered. "I wasn't sure you liked pink."

Mattie stared at him. "You mean *you* gave it to me?" She couldn't believe it. "And the ring? And the candies? And the daffodils?"

Jeb just grinned. It wasn't such a bad grin, Mattie thought. At least it wasn't green today. Then Jeb pulled her pigtail and bolted for the bus.

2. Kid for Sale—Any Amount

On the first morning of spring vacation, Mattie couldn't tie her high-top tennis shoes. Her shoelaces were missing. She felt inside her shoes but turned up only three pebbles and some lint. She looked in the washing machine, on the clothesline, and in her sock drawer. Her shoelaces weren't anywhere. Then she peeked in Emmett's room. Emmett was making spaghetti. He was pouring tomato sauce over Mattie's new, extra-long, lemon-yellow shoelaces. They were now the color of sweet potatoes. What a way to start a vacation.

On Tuesday, Emmett pulled all the tape out of Mattie's "Peter and the Wolf" cassette while Mattie was organizing her rock collection.

"What did you do that for?" Mattie shrieked.

"Wolf, come out!" Emmett shouted at the cassette.

On Wednesday, Emmett traded Mattie's gerbil, Alvin, for a cherry Popsicle.

"You're the worst little brother in the whole world!" Mattie screamed.

Emmett sucked his thumb.

Mattie's mother patted Emmett's head. "Be patient, Mattie," she said. "Emmett's too little to know any better."

But Mattie knew better. She knew when enough was enough. Today she had to get a haircut, but tomorrow she would sell him.

On Thursday, Mattie made this sign:

KID FOR SALE

EMMETT

3 YEARS OLD

ANY AMOUNT

She crossed her fingers for good luck. Then she told her sister that she and

Emmett were going to play outside. That was fine with Abby. When she babysat, she always sent them outside anyway.

But no one wanted to buy Emmett. . . .

Not the bus driver. "You don't need the right change," Mattie told her. "You can pay me later." But the driver just waved and drove away.

Not the garbage collector. "Fifty bottle caps will buy this little kid!" Mattie shouted. But he only shook his head and hopped onto the truck.

Not the dog groomer from the Pretty Pup Salon. "I'll trade him for the Pekingese," Mattie begged. The dog growled. So did the groomer.

Not even nice old Mrs. Schwartz, who liked kids a lot. "He's yours, today only, for a dozen peanut-butter cookies," said Mattie. But Mrs. Schwartz only smiled and said she hadn't baked lately.

No one wanted Emmett until Miss Abercromby passed by.

"He'll do just fine," said Miss Abercromby. "I hope five dollars is enough."

"A whole five dollars?" said Emmett.

"That's just right!" said Mattie. "Thank you very much. I hope you like him."

Miss Abercromby gave Mattie a five-dollar bill and took Emmett's hand.

Mattie could hardly believe her good luck. She had sold him! No more spaghetti shoelaces. No more wrecked tapes. No more traded pets. Life was pest-free. *And she was rich!*

Mattie skipped down the sidewalk to the drugstore. She could buy lots of candy—and she wouldn't have to share it! She grabbed two packs of baseball cards with bubble gum, a small box of chocolates with creamy middles, and three red licorice loops.

Mr. Johnson handed her three dollars in change. "Emmett will think you're his fairy godmother, Mattie."

Mattie stared at the bag of candy. "Emmett . . . ," she mumbled. "Yep. Emmett loves surprises."

At the dime store, Mattie picked out some purple yarn. Mrs. Wilson put it in a bag. "What are you making, dear?" she asked.

"A 'do not disturb' sign for my bedroom door," Mattie told her.

Mrs. Wilson winked. "To keep out a little brother, I bet."

"Well . . . ," Mattie began, swallowing her gum. "I . . . I've changed my mind. I think I'll sew purple flowers on my jeans instead." She bolted for the door so fast that she forgot to say good-bye.

With her last dollar, Mattie bought an Ace Flyer kite.

Amanda Krenshaw was buying Pink Satin nail polish. "My brother and I have Mylar box kites," she said.

"Big deal," said Mattie. She wondered if Miss Abercromby liked kites. She knew Emmett did.

Mattie sat down on the curb. Leaves swirled in the water trickling down the gutter. She liked to launch leaf boats on this small stream. She used flat, wide leaves for her boats, with twigs for masts and leaves threaded over them for the sails. After big rains, she made bigger boats from newspaper. She folded it like a hat, except turned in at the corners. She watched them skim along the water. Emmett liked to race alongside.

"Catch the boat, Emmett," she'd say. Emmett would splash and pounce—if he were there. But Emmett was at Miss Abercromby's. Did Miss Abercromby like to make paper boats too?

Mattie carefully unwrapped a chocolate. She pressed and smoothed its orange foil wrapper. She saved wrappers like this for Emmett's collages. The shiny pieces of foil made his pictures look fancy, like something for Christmas. Sometimes he made one for her as a present. She wished she could give him this wrapper—orange was his favorite color. Did Miss Abercromby know that?

Did Miss Abercromby know that Emmett ate weird food? How could she know

that he loved peanut butter and green (with the red stuff) olive sandwiches? Or that he liked syrup on his French fries?

"Emmett needs me!" Mattie jumped to her feet. "I'll give him one more chance. I'll get him back!" Then she sat right down again. She had already spent Miss Abercromby's money. How could she get Emmett back?

Mattie propped her chin on her hands and thought harder than she had ever thought before.

"One," she said, sticking up her thumb. "Buy him back." But Mattie never had five dollars all at once except right after her birthday. Even her emergency coin collection was low—a 1964 D-Mint penny and one 1987 nickel. Six cents. Anyway, she would only spend her coin collection to save a life or buy a dog.

Mattie raised her pointer finger. "Two. Get him returned." She could tell Miss Abercromby that Emmett wasn't really her brother, after all. That he had run away from his parents, and now they had forgiven him and wanted him back. But where would Mattie find the parents?

"Three." Middle finger. "Kidnap him." Tonight she could climb up Miss Abercromby's trellis, slip through Emmett's window, and sneak out again with Emmett. But where would Emmett be sleeping? It would be dark, and Emmett had broken Mattie's flashlight. What if she kidnapped Miss Abercromby by mistake?

"Four," she mumbled, lifting her ring finger. "Beg or borrow." Grandma always gave her a quarter when she went to visit. Instead of getting them one at a time for the next two years, Mattie could ask for them all at once. But Grandma would want to know why.

"Are you going to buy someone a present, honey?" she would ask. Mattie couldn't tell her, "No, Grandma. I'm going to buy Emmett."

"Five." Pinky. "Go into business." She could sell Emmett's stuff and use the money to buy him back. Miss Abercromby had bought *him,* so someone might buy his junk. He wasn't even around to miss it. But he'd be around when she bought him back. Would she have to buy his stuff back then? That would be a problem.

Mattie stood up and kicked a rock clear across the street. It bounced off the curb and stopped. "That's it!" Mattie shouted. "My rock collection!" Finally, a plan.

Mattie crossed her fingers as Miss Abercromby inspected the heavy package. She shook it, she patted it, she sniffed it. She put her ear up to it and listened to it. "I guess it won't bite," she said. She peeled off the stick-on bow and untaped the superhero wrapping paper.

"A rock!" said Miss Abercromby. "You thought I'd trade Emmett for a rock?"

"But it's a special rock," Mattie explained. "I found it at the seashore. That's why I painted it green, like seaweed. See the little gulls I painted up here?"

"Humph!" said Miss Abercromby. "I already have rocks from the sea, and rocks from the forest, and rocks from the mountains. I have too many rocks. But I don't have another Emmett!"

Mattie trudged home with her rock. She pushed open the back door. What would she tell her sister? But Abby didn't ask where Emmett was. In fact, she didn't even come to the door. Where was she? Under headphones? In the bathroom? Phew—on the telephone.

Mattie tiptoed up the stairs to her room. What else could she trade for Emmett? It had to be something Miss Abercromby did not already have. Seashells? No—Miss Abercromby had been to the seashore. Candy? No—Miss Abercromby probably never ate anything that was bad for her. Stuffed animals? Maybe her fluffy coyote or her velour snake? Hmmm. . . . Better yet, a real pet!

Mattie lifted Juliet from the aquarium. "Miss Abercromby will love you," she said. "I'm *sure* she doesn't have a salamander." She crossed her fingers and headed back to Miss Abercromby's.

"Juliet is very friendly," said Mattie.

"Yuck!" said Miss Abercromby. "Salamanders aren't smart enough to be friendly. Besides, I can't bake Juliet a chocolate-chip cookie, now, can I? That's Emmett's favorite kind, you know."

Mattie sighed. A rock wasn't good enough. A pet wasn't good enough. Just what would Miss Abercromby want? Besides Emmett, that is. Maybe something *useful*. Miss Abercromby probably liked useful stuff.

Mattie ran all the way home and straight to the garage. She dug her fishing-tackle box out of the back corner. There wasn't much tackle in it, but what was there was useful. Crossing her fingers, she ran all the way back to Miss Abercromby's.

"Will you trade Emmett for these?" She handed Miss Abercromby a red-and-white bobber and a rainbow-trout spinner. "They make nice earrings if you don't fish."

Miss Abercromby shook her head. "Are you crazy? I'd be giving up the best fishing

buddy I'll ever have. Emmett and I will do fine with worms, thank you."

Mattie tried a paper-flower lei from Hawaii next. "You could dance the hula, like this." She rolled her hips and waved her arms.

"How foolish I'd look!" said Miss Abercromby. "Besides, Emmett just taught me the hokeypokey."

Then Mattie tried a bottle of rose-hip bath oil. "You'd be as smooth as a seal," she said.

"I'd rather be a person," said Miss Abercromby.

Mattie was losing hope. She walked to the park and plopped on a bench. She stared at the sky. She wished an idea would drop on her like rain. But there was nothing up there except a red-and-yellow kite floating above the trees. She'd be better off far away, too. Without Emmett, how could she go home?

The kite was dropping now. Would it get caught in the trees? Mattie held her breath. An idea was coming. Did Miss

Abercromby have a kite? It was worth a try. "Hang on, Emmett!" she shouted, crossing her fingers over her heart.

Mattie rang Miss Abercromby's bell twice.

"What is it this time?" said Miss Abercromby.

Mattie handed her the new Ace Flyer kite. "You might as well have this," she said. "I bought it with your money."

"What a snazzy kite!" said Miss Abercromby. "Now, Mattie, I just *might* trade Emmett for that kite if only I knew how to fly it."

"How to fly it?" Mattie repeated. "Emmett and I can fly a kite as high as any bird. We can teach you right now!"

So Miss Abercromby and Mattie and Emmett went to the park. Miss Abercromby took a bag of chocolate-chip cookies along. They ate them under a swishing willow tree.

"Feels like a good kite wind," said Miss Abercromby.

"Perfect," said Mattie. "It's launch time."

Single-file, they marched up the sledding hill. Mattie was first, with the kite. Miss Abercromby carried the spool of kite string. Emmett carried the flapping tail.

The kite tugged at Mattie's arm. Miss Abercromby waited for the signal. "Let the string out slowly," Mattie shouted.

Miss Abercromby got the kite off the ground. Mattie got it over the bushes. Miss Abercromby got it above the willow tree. Mattie got it higher than the giant oak. Then Emmett brought it down into a mud puddle.

"Uh-oh," said Miss Abercromby. "Are you sure you want him back?"

"That was our deal," said Mattie. "And you get the kite."

3. The Haircut

So far, this was the best summer Mattie could remember. The Mystery Club had its first meeting in June. Darcy was president because her name was first in the alphabet. Jeb was vice-president, Lenny was treasurer, and Mattie was secretary.

Then Darcy and Lenny had to go on vacation with their families, so the club hadn't solved any mysteries yet. In fact, they hadn't even found a mystery to solve. But Mattie didn't mind. She and Jeb were building a clubhouse in the oak tree in Mattie's backyard. By the time Darcy and Lenny got back at the end of July, it would be finished. In a new treehouse, they would be sure to find some mysteries.

"Wait till Lenny gets back," said Jeb.

"He won't believe this lookout. I can see the whole block." He peered through the branches at the Krenshaws' backyard.

Mattie looked through the branches and down at the ground. She couldn't believe what she saw, either.

"C'mon, Jeb," she said. "Emmett's in trouble."

"Oooh, Emmett," said Jeb. "How did it get in your hair?"

Emmett stared at the grass. "I stuck it on my pillow at nap time." He tugged at the gooey bubble gum tangled in his hair—two Bazookas, at least.

"We'll fix it, Emmett," said Mattie. "Right, Jeb?"

"Right," said Jeb. "Shampoo will clean it all out, Emmett."

Mattie went inside to get supplies. Then she led Emmett over to the oak tree. "Right this way to the Tree House Salon," she said. "If you look good, so do we."

"First we have to wet your hair," said

Jeb. "That's how my mom does it." He aimed the garden hose at Emmett's head and blasted.

"Too hard!" cried Emmett.

"You have to be gentle, Jeb," said Mattie. She trickled water from the hose over Emmett's hair. Then she lifted the plastic bottle of shampoo over his head and squeezed.

The cap came off. Shampoo came pouring out. In half a second, Emmett's head looked like an oil slick.

"That should be enough," said Mattie. "Dig in, Jeb."

They scrubbed and rubbed until Emmett's head was a cloud of suds. His face disappeared. "I can't see!" he yelled. "My eyes!"

Mattie scooped the suds off his face and wiped his eyes. Emmett cried. "Shhh," Mattie said. "We'll fix everything." Then she rubbed his head some more.

"Brother," she moaned, "is this ever sticky."

"Yeah," said Jeb. "And I think it's

spreading. We better rinse and have a look."

Jeb squirted Emmett with the hose. "Almost done," said Jeb. Then he and Mattie stared at Emmett's dripping head. The bubble gum wasn't in one spot anymore. It was everywhere!

"Now what do we do?" said Jeb.

Mattie shrugged. "Give him a haircut?"

"You can't cut my hair!" cried Emmett. "You don't know how."

"Sure we do," said Mattie. "I've watched Dad cut your hair plenty of times. And once I saw a lady cut Mom's hair."

"Besides," said Jeb, "we've both had lots of haircuts. We're experts at it."

"What do we need?" asked Mattie.

"A comb and brush, scissors, my dad's clippers . . ." Jeb really did sound like an expert.

"And a ruler," said Mattie. "So it's even."

Jeb ran home to get the stuff. Mattie stayed with Emmett.

"It'll be all right," she kept telling him.

But a big tear rolled down Emmett's cheek anyway.

When Jeb got back, Mattie measured. "It's three inches long at the top," she said. "If we cut one inch off all around, that ought to do it. You take his left side, Jeb. I'll take his right."

"It's hard to measure a clump of hair with gum in it," said Jeb. *Whack.*

"I think you cut higher over his ear than I did," said Mattie. *Snip.*

"I can cut out this hunk all at once," said Jeb. *Chop.*

"One more bunch up here, and it's all gone," said Mattie. *Hack hack.*

"There's still some gum in this spot," said Jeb. He turned the clippers on. "I'll shave it." *Bzzzzzzzz.*

"That's it!" said Mattie. She stood back to look. Every trace of gum was gone. There was only one problem: Emmett's head looked like a pineapple.

"Let me see!" said Emmett.

Mattie crossed her fingers behind her back. "First we have to style it."

"Uh, right," said Jeb.

Mattie went inside to get the supplies—hair spray, gel, a mirror, Vaseline. She ran out and bowed to Emmett. "Hello. I'm Mattie, your stylist."

Mattie slicked. Jeb sprayed. Mattie combed Emmett's hair forward. Jeb combed it backward. They both combed it sideways. It still looked awful.

Then Emmett grabbed the mirror. "Where's my hair?" he wailed.

Jeb pointed to the ground.

"Put it back!" said Emmett.

"That's a great idea," said Mattie. "We'll rearrange it." She spread a sticky tuft of hair over a bald spot. Jeb stuck one clump back on and then another. They both patched, smoothed, and patted until Emmett's hair was all back on his head.

Emmett snatched up the mirror. "Noooo," he moaned. He was right. A scarecrow in a tornado looked better than this.

Jeb took off his baseball cap. He handed

it to Emmett. "Put this on," he said. "You can wear it till your hair grows back."

"At least we got the gum out," said Mattie.

That night Emmett wore his cap to bed.

"Jeb gave it to him, Mom," Mattie explained. "You know how little kids are." Especially when they're almost bald, she thought.

When the lights were out, Emmett crawled into Mattie's bed.

"How long will it take?" he asked.

"For what?" said Mattie.

"For my hair to grow back," said Emmett.

Mattie didn't know how fast hair grew, but she was sure it wasn't fast enough. "It depends if it's the fast-growing kind or the slow-growing kind," she said. "Maybe we'll know in the morning." She crossed her fingers under her pillow.

At breakfast Emmett made oatmeal mountains in his cereal bowl.

"Eat up, Emmett," said Mom. "It'll put hair on your chest."

"Wrong place," Mattie mumbled.

"And take off your cap," said Mom. "We don't wear our hats at the table."

Emmett shook his head. Mom reached for the cap. Mattie held her breath. Emmett slipped under the table and dashed out the back door.

"Now what's got into him?" asked Mom.

"Don't know," said Mattie.

"Go find him," said Mom.

Emmett wasn't in his sandbox. He wasn't visiting the Krenshaws' pet rabbit. He wasn't at Jeb's house, either.

"He's run away," Mattie told Jeb. "He thought his hair would grow back overnight. We've *got* to find him."

"Let's go!" said Jeb.

They searched in Mr. Kickernick's garden. They looked behind Mrs. Blume's woodpile. They checked in everybody's window wells. No Emmett.

They rang the doorbells up and down the block—even Miss Abercromby's.

"First you sold him. Then you traded him back. And now you've lost him?" said Miss Abercromby. But she gave them three chocolate-chip cookies anyway. "One's for Emmett," she said. "Make sure you don't eat it."

Mattie stuffed the cookies into her pocket. Then she and Jeb searched the park. Still no Emmett. They asked the ice-cream man, "Have you seen a little kid with shaggy hair?" He hadn't.

"If only I hadn't told him that his hair might grow back fast," said Mattie.

"If only we hadn't cut his hair," said Jeb.

"Where would *you* go with hair like his?" Mattie asked.

"To the barbershop?" said Jeb.

"It's worth a try," said Mattie.

Ken's Klip and Kut was just two blocks away, at the other side of St. Luke's School.

"That's weird," said Jeb.

"What?" asked Mattie.

"Who'd hang out in a school playground in the summer?"

Mattie stared through the chain-link fence. The heat sizzled off the playground blacktop. The bike rack was empty. The swings stood stock-still. Just one person was there. A little person lying head down at the bottom of the slide. A little person named *Emmett!*

Mattie raced to the gate and onto the playground. "Emmett!" she yelled. "What are you doing?"

"I'm growing my hair faster," said Emmett.

"Hanging upside down won't help," said Mattie.

Emmett looked heartbroken.

"It might," said Jeb. "I run faster down a hill than up." He rubbed Emmett's hair. "I think it's working already."

"Really?" asked Emmett.

Mattie smiled. She crossed her fingers behind her back. "Jeb's right," she said.

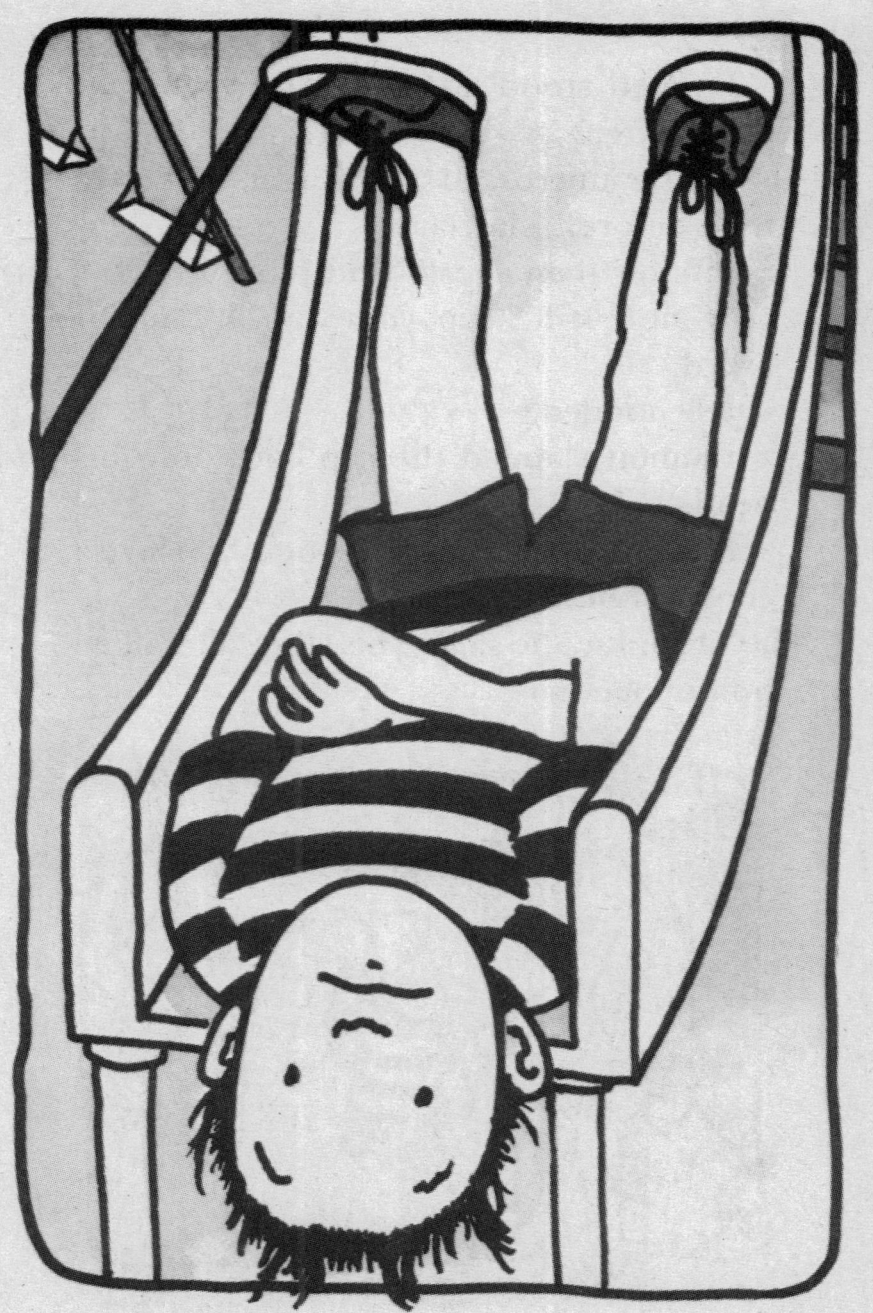

Emmett stood up. "Does my hair *really* look better?"

Mattie uncrossed her fingers. "Better than before," she said.

"Better than ever!" said Jeb.

"Can I still keep your cap?" Emmett asked.

Jeb nodded.

Emmett slapped the cap back onto his head.

Mattie reached into her pocket. "Have a cookie, Emmett."

"Thanks," he said. Then they all walked home together.